YOUR KNOWLEDGE HAS VALUE

Massimo Santanicchia

The Life and Death of Great American Suburbs

Political and Social Consequences of fifty years of Sub-Urbanisation

GRIN Verlag

Bibliografische Information der Deutschen Nationalbibliothek:

Die Deutsche Bibliothek verzeichnet diese Publikation in der Deutschen National-
bibliografie; detaillierte bibliografische Daten sind im Internet über http://dnb.d-
nb.de/ abrufbar.

Imprint:

Copyright © 2002 GRIN Verlag GmbH
Druck und Bindung: Books on Demand GmbH, Norderstedt Germany
ISBN: 978-3-656-41354-7

This book at GRIN:

http://www.grin.com/en/e-book/212646/the-life-and-death-of-great-american-
suburbs

GRIN - Your knowledge has value

Der GRIN Verlag publiziert seit 1998 wissenschaftliche Arbeiten von Studenten, Hochschullehrern und anderen Akademikern als eBook und gedrucktes Buch. Die Verlagswebsite www.grin.com ist die ideale Plattform zur Veröffentlichung von Hausarbeiten, Abschlussarbeiten, wissenschaftlichen Aufsätzen, Dissertationen und Fachbüchern.

Visit us on the internet:

http://www.grin.com/

http://www.facebook.com/grincom

http://www.twitter.com/grin_com

The Life and Death
of Great American Suburbs

Political and Social Consequences of fifty years of Sub-Urbanisation

Massimo Santanicchia | May 2002

Introduction

"Our property seems to me the most beautiful in the world. It is so close to Babylon that we enjoy all the advantages of the city, and yet when we come home we are away from the noise and dust". Written in cuneiform on a clay tablet, this letter to the King of Persia in 539 B.C. represents the first extant expression of the suburban ideal. (K. T. Jackson 1985)

2600 years later in the United States things have slightly changed; our property might still appears as the most beautiful in the world but we do not have to go to the city anymore to benefit from all the advantages of this. The "advantages" instead have moved themselves outside the city centres to constitute what Peter G. Rowe calls the "middle landscape", a heterogeneous entity that lies between the city and the countryside.

What are the social and political consequences of the "middle landscape" today?

The creation of the American suburb

Suburbia for K.T. Jackson has become the quintessential physical achievement of the United States. "Suburbia symbolises the fullest, most unadulterated embodiment of contemporary culture; it is a manifestation of such fundamental characteristics of American society as conspicuous consumption, reliance upon the private automobile, upward mobility, the separation of the family into nuclear units, the widening division between work and leisure, and a tendency toward racial and economic exclusiveness"[1].

But were American people really free in their choice for suburbia?

There are definitely strong cultural influences that have favoured a return of people to the countryside. Intellectuals as Beecher, Downing and Vaux were part of an Anglo-American culture that had never placed a high value on city life; they have always talked about home rather than community (K. T. Jackson 1985).

"Around 1850 many suburban neighbourhoods were developed in the Unites States. They were places for the upper class like the one designed by Frederick Law Olmstead, Riverside in the outskirt of Chicago and linked to it by a commuter railway. Everything was planned, the water supply, drainage, schools and recreational facilities and set aside seven hundred acres for public use."[2]

With the extension of the wealth to a broader amount of people, the phenomenon of sub-urbanisation became more visible. It became not just important to move outside the city but to your own land and house, to fulfil that ideal of perfect combination between country and city that was already expressed in the ancient Babylon.

The single-family dwelling became the paragon of middle-class housing, the most visible symbol of having arrived at a fixed place in society, the goal to which every decent family aspired. (K. T. Jackson 1985)

---

[1] Jackson, Kenneth T., Crabgrass Frontier, Oxford University press, 1985
[2] Jackson, Kenneth T., Crabgrass Frontier, Oxford University press, 1985

The technological development then made possible to cover broader distances on a daily base. As K. T. Jackson explains between 1815 and 1875, America's largest cities underwent a dramatic spatial change. The introduction of the steam ferry, the omnibus, the commuter railroad, the horse car, the elevated railroad, and the cable car inaugurate a new pattern of suburban affluence.

At the turn of the 19th century, the electric streetcar represented a revolutionary advance in transportation technology. Radiating outward from the central business districts, the tracks opened up a vast suburban ring that grew in tandem with the extension of the public transportation.

A "new city" segregated by class and economic functions and encompassing an area triple the territory of the older walking city, had clearly emerged as the centre of the American urban society. (K. T. Jackson 1985)

After World War I, suburban growth was shaped by automobiles, which became the second icon of the suburban life: cars provided and unprecedented level of mobility, freeing people to determine their own travel patterns, and strengthened the suburbs' middle class nature by excluding those who could not afford it.

By that time everybody was fascinated by these modern miracles, nobody raised the question of what would have been their social and political consequences.

"Happiness was often equated with the satisfaction of material needs, and technocratic know-how was seen to be omnipotent, quickly overcoming mundane problems of contemporary life, such as urban blight and traffic congestion" (Akin 1977, Corn 1986)

Still by that time Americans were able to choose where they would have fancied living. The great shift happened around the 1930s.

"The new deal"

As K.T. Jackson and Andrew Ross affirm the post war formula for mass sub-urbanisation emerged from the pressure of a powerful coalition of real estate, finance, and transportation interests. It also included the oil, asphalt, and rubber industries, tire manufactures and dealers, motorbus operators, parts suppliers, road builders, state highway administrators, service-station owners, and many other groups that pursued their common interests as the America Road Builders Association (ARBA).

In 1943 the ARBA with General Motors as the largest contributor, formed a lobby second only to the munitions industry.

After the war, the vested interests of these groups meshed with the federal need to create jobs and provide affordable shelter for over 16 million returning vets.

When the Federal Housing Administration FHA guaranteed bankers' loans to builders, and Veteran Administration VA offered low interest mortgages as part of the GI Bill of Rights, vets could virtually borrow the entire value of a home without a down payment. Soon buying a house become cheaper than renting one, thanks to long-term, low-interest mortgage. The result, if not the intent of Washington programs have been to encourage decentralisation. While it was a national purpose to build subsidised highways and utilities outside of cities, it was not national policy to help cities repairing and rebuilding aging transit systems, bridges, streets, and water and sewer lines.

Thus, sub-urbanisation was not an historical inevitability created by geography, technology, and culture, but rather the product of a "new deal" between government policies and the America Road Builders Association lobby. (K. T. Jackson 1985)

Social engineering was then a crucial, and immoral, part of the sub-urbanisation scheme. "In the name of neighbourhood security, the FHA adopted the Home Owners Loan Corporation's codes governing racial zoning, especially its secret ratings categories for valuing neighbourhoods and blocks according to racial homogeneity"[3]

By that time Americans lost their right to choose between suburb and city.

Levittown

With these premises the suburb of Levittown took place.

Abraham Levitt and his sons, William and Alfred built more than 140,000 houses and turned a cottage industry into a major manufacturing process. In 1946 they bought 4,000 acres of potato farms in the town of Hempsted, Long Island where they planned the biggest private housing project in American history: Levittown.

The construction was industrialised and divided up in twenty-seven distinct steps: beginning with laying the foundation and ending with a clean sweep for the new home. This made possible the construction of more than thirty houses each day, or one every sixteen working minutes.

Ultimately encompassing more than 17,400 separate houses and 82,000 residents, Levittown was the largest housing development ever put up by a single builder.

"This post war American New Town may be considered as primarily engineering structures not only due to their direct technical descent from World War II typologies, but because their central planning rationality is directed in an entirely new way: they are primarily business enterprises run by private corporations and therefore subject to modern accounting practices."[4]

As Keller Easterling notices: "Levittown is not a town or community but rather a large tract of privately owned land overlaid with curving streets and a platting plan".

A second Levittown was then built few years later in Pennsylvania.

"There were three basic house types costing from $11,500 to $14,500. A collection of such houses would have been merely a "subdivision". What made it a "community" was that for each cluster of twelve hundred units or so, there was an elementary school, a playground, and a swimming pool. Not only that, but a complex of ten or twelve such "neighbourhoods" was complemented by a large shopping centre, some smaller ones, high schools, a library and parks, some of which were provided

---

[3] Ross, Andrew, The Celebration Chronicles, Verso, London, 2000
[4] Francine Fort, Michel Jacques (ed), Mutations, Actar, Barcelona, 2001

by the builder himself. It was no less than an attempt to create from scratch what the builder honestly and open-mindedly thought was the entire range of local institutions and facilities found in the old communities that people were enthusiastically leaving." (Joel Garreau 1991)

The "Edge City"

"Between 1950 and 1970, the suburban population doubled from 36 to 74 million, and 83% of the nation's total growth took place in the suburbs.
In 1970, for the first time in the history of the world, a nation-state counted more suburbanites than city dwellers or farmers."[5]
Joel Garreau describes this new reality with the name of "Edge City". For him the middle landscape has nothing to do with the previous downtown or with the vision of the suburb as a bedroom community.
"Within the middle landscape shaped out of the suburban mosaic, society is becoming as heterogeneous and life is becoming as diversified as they were once in the city".[6]
"Our edge cities are tied together not by locomotives and subways, but by freeways, jet ways, and jogging paths. Their characteristic monument is not a horse-mounted hero in the square, but an atrium shielding trees perpetually in leaf at the cores of our corporate headquarters, fitness centres, and shopping plazas. Our new urban centres are marked not by the penthouses of the old urban rich, or the tenements of the old urban poor, but by the celebrated single family home with grass all around."[7]
As K.T. Jackson noticed in the 1980s these kinds of houses constituted two-thirds of the 86.4 million dwelling units in the Unites States.

The consequences of this way of "urbanising" are multiples.
From an ecological point of view 50 acres of prime farmland every hour of every day are lost to development[8].
Economically then, the cost of maintaining the infrastructures of the low-density suburban housing formula have begun to outstrip the budgets of middle-class residents and tax-starved local governments. For instance an average American family spends one-sixth of its total budget on transportation, more than on food, clothing, or healthcare. (Andrew Ross 2000)
Finally, there are political and social consequences.

The political and social consequences

The middle landscape has erased the spatial contexts (public streets, squares and plazas) that have made possible for centuries the mingling of the different social groups, which is at the base of the public sphere.

---

[5] Jackson, Kenneth T., Crabgrass Frontier, Oxford University press, 1985
[6] Rowe, Peter G., Making a Middle Landscape, The MIT Press Cambridge, Massachusetts, 1991
[7] Garreau, Joel, Edge City, life on the new frontier, Anchor Books, 1991
[8] Francine Fort, Michel Jacques (ed), Mutations, Actar, Barcelona, 2001

According to Paul Hirst the privatisation of the public space is not just wanted by private corporations through shopping malls, network of enclosed urban walkways as in Toronto, but it is also driven by the fears of the middle class of the "danger" of the streets.

The response is to create a spatial system of social segregation, excluding the poor and the non-Anglo from the private non-city. Today nine million American people live in gated communities, cities as Atlantis in Florida spends 70% of its budget on guards and gates. (Francine Fort 2001)

The result is to marginalize the city streets and to make them dangerous, leaving them to the excluded, whereas we need truly open spaces where the plural groups of the modern city can meet, mix and recognise one another.

The street is the classical locus of publicity, because it is also the site of openness and equality. That's why it is so important to preserve the public space because the open communication is the foundation of the true democracy.

The everyday co-mingling and commerce of social groups is the basis of an equality of social membership that makes possible a common policy. (Paul Hirst, 2002)

The "New Urbanism" and the question of identity

With these premises a movement called "the New Urbanism" has been trying since the late 1970s to repair the consequences of the sprawl, working instead with a compact close-knit community.

Conceptually the New Urbanism aims at neighbourhood communities based on a pedestrian system and with a clear end of the built area, while, the circulation on a regional scale should be mainly based on public transports. Finally, civic and private domains should form a complementary hierarchy.

All these points are extremely important; nations as The Netherlands, Denmark, and Sweden have been working in this direction for many years.

Why then in the United States, are the New Urbanism's principles applied to resort towns as Seaside or to experimental communities as Celebration (that seems to be more of a club than of a city)?

And why these towns have to look like old American communities?

Why the answer for twenty-first-century cities has to be a radical return to the nineteenth century? (Joel Garreau 1991)

In Seaside planned in 1980 by Andres Duany and Elizabeth Plater-Zyberk the symbolism is inescapable.

We are almost literally taken back to the nineteenth century, and this of course raises questions about cultural authenticity.

Questions of identity and feelings of alienation are modern dilemmas in our growing metropolitan areas; when a sense of cultural community is threatened, stylistic eclecticism often results. (Peter G. Rowe 1991)

It is true indeed that a number of causes are contributing to the decomposition of an ethnically and culturally homogeneous society of the kind nation-states have sought to construct. But why this social change has to be accompanied by rhetoric about "identity under threat".

The question of identity seems to have reached a very important issue.
Now that markets and financial networks are increasingly independent of state boundaries, more and more often people re-claim their sense of identity in the meaning of distinctiveness.
According to Manuel Castells, the age of globalisation is also the age of nationalist resurgence, expressed both in the challenge to established nation-states and in the widespread (re) construction of identity on the basis of nationality, always affirmed against the alien.
But one cannot respond to such changes nostalgically, by seeking to rebuild the classical city (Paul Hirst 2002).
One cannot hide the multicultural reality of America behind the same 19th century façade: it is fake!
For Richard Sennett a community is more than a set of customs, behaviour, or attitudes about other people. A community is also a collective identity; it is a way of saying who we are.

The ex-urban and post-public period

For Michael Sorkin the American society is going through a problematic period defined as ex-urban and post-public.
One of the first elements that are shaping the American society is the weakening of the nation-state and the city as its municipal complement as decision-makers in the community.
Nation-states have been losing salience since the early 1970s, as the renewed internationalisation of economic relations has limited the capacities of national economical management. We are today dealing with a multi-located political world with complex and overlapping governing powers, some multi-national, some national and some non-state. We shall need to get used to the idea of direct government by international agencies in certain areas of policy, and of "community" self government for certain purposes (Paul Hirst 2002).

Celebration

Celebration, the town created by Disney Company in 1995 is expected to host more than 20,000 residents in the next decades, is a perfect example of self-managed place.
"The reason of Celebration is rooted in the repulsion for the existing order of things"[9].
Most Celebratrionites were attracted to the efficiency of private government.
Many have lost faith in public institutions and public government, and described democratic public process as laborious, wasteful, and inept. (Andrew Ross 2000)

---

[9] Ross, Andrew, The Celebration Chronicles, Verso, London, 2000

"Celebration is clearly governed by a corporation, rather than a government, and so what happens is that American corporations are treating you as a customer. A customer is possibly treated better than a citizen in this country"[10]

In Celebration you do not simply buy a house, you buy a package that includes education, high technology, unequalled health facilities and quality home, you buy a dream, tailored made to fulfil your wishes.

"Marketing studies help to perpetuate a set of needs and desires that replaces the American tradition with a fiction about home and civic life that can be pack-aged and sold".[11]

The builders say: "We are going to build this thing that is perfect for you. We haven't met you but we know what you're like and we know you're going to like it here"
(Joel Garreau)

But as Peter Eisenman has noted: "There would never be any change in the world if we always gave people what they want, because what they want is what they know, not what is unknown. An architect's role, or one of the traditional roles of architecture, is to mirror change, to reflect the possibility for change and to act critically on it."

What the architects have tried to do in the last twenty years in America has been to create a community, maybe because the State has been unable to do it.

"Community" has become a competitive feature in the consumer housing industry, where developers bundle it into the package of amenities on offer.

"Celebration's planners set out to raise the bar in the industry by offering a deluxe next-generation version of the all-inclusive community package, far beyond the "enclaving" model that promised a safe retreat from the city. Celebration's packaging was expected to set the new standard for community-in-depth models of marketing."[12]

All of this take the shape of a neo-traditional town, again the hope in the future is visualised in a return to the past.

"The first Levittown, as Herbert Gans pointed out, was neither a town (which would offer employment) nor a community (which suggests a desire for sharing values).

The Levittowners moved there to own a house, most of them for the first time in their lives. Celebration did not yet feel like a town, but it was conceived and populated with the aim of becoming a community as quickly as possible"[13]

But can one create a community when even the plant's species in ones garden is decided for you (as it is in Celebration)? Does community mean creating a synthetic space?
It is also a lack of respect and faith in everybody's choices.

Faux notes. "It is a vision of total safety, where every need is met. It is an egomaniac's version of what a community would do to itself if it had the time. It's spooky. It's false. It is predictable, not real. It is not what a community builds. There are no little mom-and-pop stores. Parks are used as buffers.

---

[10] Ross, Andrew, The Celebration Chronicles, Verso, London, 2000
[11] Easterling, Keller (ed.), Seaside making a town in America, Princeton Architectural Press, New York 1991,
[12] Ross, Andrew, The Celebration Chronicles, Verso, London, 2000
[13] Ross, Andrew, The Celebration Chronicles, Verso, London, 2000

Their function has been changed. They are not places for people to congregate; they are places to keep people at bay." (Joel Garreau 1991)

Disney produces fiction that in its virtuality can therefore be perfect; here instead we are dealing with reality and reality is problematic.
Because of all the problems emerged in the management of Celebration, Disney Company withdrew its brand from the town in the summer 1997.

In America a customer can be better treated than a citizen but the "shop" can always close down!

From enclaves to multiple forums

In 1961 Lewis Mumford said in his analysis of "The City in the History":
"In the mass movement into suburban areas a new kind of community was produced, which caricatured both the historic city and the archetypical suburban refuge: a multitude of uniform, unidentifiable houses, lined up inflexibly, at uniform distances, on uniform roads, in a treeless communal waste, inhabited by people of the same class, the same income, the same age group, witnessing the same television performances, eating the same tasteless pre-fabricated foods, from the same freezers, conforming in every outward and inward respect to a common mold, manufactured in the central metropolis. Thus, the ultimate effect of the suburban escape in our own time is, ironically, a low-grade uniform environment from which escape is impossible."

In the time between the building of the Levittowns and the founding of Celebration, the middle landscape of suburbia has sprouted a hundred different species of developments and undergone some significant population shifts.
By the time of the 1990 census, a third of all African Americans (Levittown for instance was excluded to black people for more than two decades after the war) had suburban homes.
But despite the findings of Gans and others, the view of suburbia as an oppressive and alienating environment has prevailed. Those who are especially critical of suburban sprawl continue to assume that its physical disconnectedness produces residents with low moral or civic fibre. Today, the association is almost taken for granted (housing and traffic patterns determine civic personality) but it is still largely unsubstantiated.
Do cul-de-sacs, half-acre lots, and houses with garages in the front automatically produce mediocre citizens? The answer may depend, ultimately, on how you view citizenship. But those who believe that the buildings we inhabit determine our civic behaviour too often put the cart before the horse. Active citizenship has to be learned. But then one has to give this chance to people. (Andrew Ross 2000)

Maybe, as Paul Hirst says: "We must abandon the view of politics based on settled and relatively homogeneous communities, whether of nation or city."

We live in a cultural pluralism and it becomes less and less possible to provide common services to diverse groups. And when these diverse groups live in distinct enclaves a common management of them seems impossible.

One might say provocatively that if we are looking for a new political model then we should forget classical Athens and instead adopt Ottoman Damascus in which plural self-governing communities coexisted side by side.
Once we begin to think in such terms, the issue of equality must shift to ensuring that most groups and communities have the capacity and the resources for self-regulation. (Paul Hirst, 2002)

The city will cede power to functional authorities, to regional governments, and to the plural and competing self-regulating groups within it will be a less coherent entity. Municipal governments will remain for certain common functions like basic control planning, but they will shed many of their current services in areas like education and social welfare. Governments will share the space of the city with voluntary associations and cultural groups, who will also govern it. Thus there will be multiple forums and multiple spaces of public life, with individuals and communities intersecting across a far more complex and differentiated social space.
Such a world is unlikely to be equal. It will have its rich enclaves. But it need have no desperately deprived ghettos. If one were to accept the radical pluralist model and the specific forms of evening-up through community self-regulation, the "street" would matter less. (Paul Hirst, 2002)

Bibliography

Castells, Manuel, The Power of Identity, Blackwell Publishers, 1997.

Francine Fort, Michel Jacques (ed), Mutations, Actar, Barcelona, 2001

Garreau, Joel, Edge City, life on the new frontier, Anchor Books, 1991

Jackson, Kenneth T., Crabgrass Frontier, Oxford University press, 1985

Katz, Peter (ed.), The New Urbanism: Toward an Architecture of Community, McGraw-Hill, New York, 1994

Mohney, David and Easterling, Keller (ed) Seaside making a town in America, Princeton Architectural Press, New York 1991,

Ross, Andrew, The Celebration Chronicles, Verso, London, 2000

Rowe, Peter G., Making a Middle Landscape, The MIT Press Cambridge, Massachusetts, 1991

Sorkin, Michael (ed.), Variations on a Theme Park: The New American City and the End of Public Space, Hill and Wang, 1992